Black Mesa Poems

ALSO AVAILABLE
BY JIMMY SANTIAGO BACA
FROM NEW DIRECTIONS

Immigrants In Our Own Land & Selected Early Poems

Martín & Meditations on the South Valley
With an Introduction by Denise Levertov

Jimmy Santiago Baca

Black Mesa Poems

A NEW DIRECTIONS BOOK

Confluencia, Laney College Journal, Las Americas, Mothering Magazine, Mother Jones, New Kauri, New Life News, Pembroke, Puerto Del Sol, The Pushcart Prize: Best of the Small Presses 1989, Quarterly West, The Sun, and Upstream.

Some of these poems also appeared in Timberline Press's 1986 chapbook of Jimmy Santiago Baca's poetry, Poems Taken From My Yard.

Manufactured in the United States of America.
New Directions Books are printed an acid-free paper.
Published simultaneously in Canada by Penguin Books Canada Limited.
First published as New Directions Paperbook 676 in 1989.

Library of Congress Cataloging-in-Publication Data

Baca, Jimmy Santiago, 1952–
    Black Mesa poems / Jimmy Santiago Baca.
        p.   cm.—(A New Directions paperbook ; 676)
    Includes index.
    ISBN 0–8112–1102–9 (alk. paper)
    I. Title.
PS3552.A254B54   1989
811'.54—dc20
                                    89–31605
                                    CIP

FOURTH PRINTING

New Directions Books are published for James Laughlin
by New Directions Publishing Corporation
80 Eighth Avenue, New York 10011

Contents

IN LOVING MEMORY OF
TONY NARCISCO

Black Mesa Poems

DREAM COME EARLY

Odds
were astronomical,
like the field goal
Bernie kicked at Harrison Junior school,
two seconds to go, and he
booted it from the 45—
wobbling end over end, over
and through the uprights.
We won.
Others came to ask about this
leaf-cushioned house,
neighbors and newlyweds,
always denied, 'til we stopped,
asked a man walking down a dirt road,
"Who owns that house?"
"Ms. Thompson."
"Is it for sale?"
"Oh, forget it. Everyone has offered
to buy it, offering much more
than it's worth. Myself ten years now,
but she won't sell. Just won't sell."

Stooping over, rubber-gloved, tattered
sunbonnet, hoeing, lean, fully
clothed in August afternoon
against wasp bites, she rose,
lit a cigarette, leaned on her hoe.
"I own that house," her voice
a long guttural stretch of barbwire
protecting what's hers,
". . . leave your number and we'll see."

We never expected her to call,
drove off in my battered, fender-clanking

'68 Volkswagen.
                    She called.
We couldn't afford it,
but our fancy for an old adobe house,
embedded early in my wife's heart
at Sheep's Head Bay,
where as a girl
she watched Gene Autry, and fell asleep
to moons of brass doorknobs,
flagstone steps, thick bluish glasspanes,
hardwood floors,
                    swirling in the vortex with her
                    two thousand miles away,
                    I watched Zorro

and ached for a farm.
An abundance of craggy branches,
wind howling in at whiskered owls,
ruffling white hawk's throat down,
where boisterous petals
exude moist
chaos of fragrance
dizzying the nostrils,
and dazzling hums of insects
sweep coastal greens of bush-slopes,
their wings canoe oars
entangled in vines and flowers.

Knowing the house would be ours
in a month,
we drove down each dusk, lay outside
the front gate in a headlight-high grass.
We gazed up through branches of the immense
American elm, as breeze whispered in leaves
our dream had come truly early in life.

Kitchen courtyard wide, beams
blending into arches Arabic style,

walls thick as an ox's shoulder,
adobe rough-handed and rafted from the Río Grande,
wagon'd to Black Mesa
one hundred fifty years ago.
Hand-hewn floor boards smooth as cured buckskin,
tiny chips where hammer struck at board creases
are drumheads of workers, chanting, chanting—
house full of kind spirits, whose
blossoms fountain

in long-fringed leggings of buffalo dancers
at each window,
and deep bellied apricot branches
cush-cush-cush apricots
over porch, lawn and roof,
hooves of deer at night
nibbling ears of a corn patch. . . .
Lilac bushes handspring white sprays of blossoms,
and everything overbrims
neighboring green, so fenceline, telephone
and utility lines disappear, sunk fishing lines
in deep green leaf waves,
rage with fertile defiance. Each leaf,
root, blossom, submit to instinct,
in each stem and twig wild untied energy
shuffles lazily a lion of light
to pools of dew, to areas of sunlight,
and then returns to its den of darkness.

———————

Falling asleep in
the wrought-iron porch swing,
to the work rhythms of *Indios y Mejicanos*
who cut *terrón,* smooth adobe
clean as breeze pats snow
on winter nights, I drift
along this dream into my destiny.

OLD MAN

My heart was once an elementary
school-building hall
during class change, filled
with a hundred excited voices.
Fragrance of soap on my cheeks,
t-shirt blue jelly spotted, I ran
to see evening softball games,
whiffing scent of rain in the air.
The earth smelled of the new pair
of shoes mother wore
as we stood in our driveway
and waved at father
roaring away in his bright red Mack,
gone for another
three-week haul.

Each tree was a green lit window
I used as a marker when walking in the dark, when
I stayed out too late, and found myself alone.

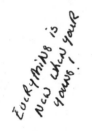

Earth was a mask, breathing
through small holes in rocks, alive,
and each evening mist swirled out dialogues
of eternities I would live.
Dawn was a white soaring torch,
that left my name a fossil
    as I became a wheel,
     a lizard,
     a roadrunner—

I do not want to become an old man.

FROM VIOLENCE TO PEACE

Twenty-eight shotgun pellets
crater my thighs, belly and groin.
I gently thumb each burnt bead,
fingering scabbed stubs with ointment.

Could have neutered me, made extinct
the volatile, romantic man I am.
"He's dead,"
doctor at emergency room
could've easily told my wife that night.
Instead, "Soak him in a bath twice a day. Apply
this ointment to the sores. Here's a month's supply
of pain killers." I remember the deep guttural groan
I gave, when the doctor pressed my groin.
        Assured
I could still make love, morphine drowsed me
and in a dull stupor I don't remember
police visiting my bed, or laughing so hard,
they scowled for a serious answer.
I howled a U.F.O. shot me along the Río Grande,
and they cursed and left.

In the summer of '88
I'd traded alfalfa for a bull calf.
Still smelling of milk udders,
I tied it to the truck rack and drove off.
Its hooves teethed
at pink roots
'til the whole lush field went bare dirt.
A magnificent bull.
Glowing wheel of heart
breathed brimming stream of white flame at dawn.
He wrangled his black brawn
like a battleshield to challenge the sun,

reared thick neck down and sideways,
lunged at me with dart and snort,
hoof-stamped and nostrilled dirt,
       'til I growled him back
       whipping air
       with a limber willow branch,
       poured grain in trough
       and spread alfalfa.
I respected his horns
and he the whistling
menace of willow.

One afternoon my cousin Patricio
helped me band the bull's scrotum,
usurp swollen sap
in his testicle sack. It withered
to a pink wattle and seeded
the garden to drive cornstalks
to bear hardy, golden horns.

Thereafter, he grazed the fenceline,
with the tempered lust and peaceful grace
of a celibate priest.
His bearing now arranged itself
elegant as a wild flower
sprung over night.

———————

Perfecto shot it.
Rasping on a black rope of blood
round its neck, it staggered,
bouldering convulsions.
Blood exploding
in bright lash of earthquaked air,
it stumble-butted stock trailer fender—
second and third shots glowed
its death.

A quivering shadow of life-flame
darkened the air and it sputtered
a last drop of blood.
I drank long swigs
of whiskey and, thinking it was dead,
turned to walk away,
then

        it gave a tremendous groan, tremendous groan,
        a birth-letting groan . . . a moon groan . . .
        blood spurted out, thick, thick, thick
        alleys of dead star blood

        and I turned and said aloud to myself,
                "That's the moon's voice!
                That's the moon's voice!"

And the white moon was in the sky,
and I looked at the moon for a long time.

———————

I sat on the ground
and gulped whiskey, drank the steer's death
still warm in my throat.
A beautiful animal! I allowed to be butchered.
When it trounced and galloped in the field,
its body was a dark, windy cliff edge,
and its eyes were doorways of a dream—
        now it bled a charred scroll
        of ancient chant in gravel, I would never know,
        and its blackened logs of blood
        smoldered dying vowels, I would never hear.
My heart's creak-n-tremble rage
milled the steer's death to red grist,
I grieved,
I wept drunkenly
that no one cared,

that humankind betrayed him,
that we were all cowards.

Perfecto, Valasquez and the butcher
tried to stop me
from driving,

> but now was the time to settle
> a bad feud with another friend.
> Redeem the bull's blood with ours.
> I drove to Felipe's house,
> anger knotted in me
> tight as the rope tied
> to the stock trailer
> steer strained against.
> I pulled, but could not free myself.
> (I had a dream night before—
> I crossed black-iron footbridge,
> partially collapsed by sea storm.
> Left-hand railing swept out to sea,
> I gripped bolt-studded right-hand railing,
> finger-clutched wire netting sides,
> carefully descended waist-high water. Waded
> through slowly and ascended other side—
> but had lost my sunglasses and wallet,
> went back, groped bottom, found them and ascended again.)

Had to cross that bridge again.
Full of significance . . . tonight,
deepest part of flooded bridge was danger . . . drowning . . .
represented years of my life collapsed
and destroyed, water the cleansing element,
my ascent from had me healed, onto firm ground,
but I went back, to re-live
destruction . . .

> "Felipe!" I yelled, porch light
> flicked on, illuminating the yard.

"Came to fight," I said, "take off
your glasses."

Bug-eyes glazed
bewildered, then gray slits of lips
snarled, "You motherless dog!"
He withdrew in darkness a moment,
reappeared on porch, serrated saw of his voice
cut the chill dark,
> "*¡Hijo de su pinche madre!*
> *¡Mátalo! ¡Mátalo!!*"

First shot framed darkness round me
with a spillway of bright light,
eruption of sound, and second shot roared
a spray of brilliance and the third
gave an expanded halo-flash.
My legs woozed, and then
I buckled to the ground.
> (I thought, holy shit, what ever happened
> to the old yard-style fight between estranged friends!)

I groaned with the steer,
and crawled my dead legs
to the truck, lunged on elbows into cab,
hand lifting the dead stone beneath my waist
to clutch and brake.

Following morning calls came,
"Tell us who did it Gato!"
"Our rifles are loaded!"
> I said,   "Leave it alone. What would you do
> if a drunk man came into your yard,
> threatened to beat you?"
I wanted peace,
wanted to diffuse the immovable core
of vengeance in my heart,
I had carried since a child,

dismantle the bloody wheel of violence
I had ridden since a child.

During my week in bed,
pellets pollinated me
with a forgotten peace,
and between waking thoughts of anger and vengeance,
sleep was a small meadow of light,
a clearing I walked into and rested. Fragrance of peace
filled me as fragrance
of flowers and dirt permeate hands
that work in the garden all day.

Curandero came to visit, and said,
"The bull in ancient times was the symbol of females.
Did you know that? Killing the bull,
is killing the intuitive part of yourself,
the feminine part. Did you realize,
when Jesus was raising Lazarus,
he groaned in his spirit and that bull groaned,
and when you killed the bull, it was raising you.
The dying bull gave birth to you and now you are either
blessed or cursed. The flood of that bull's blood,
is either going to drown you or liberate you,
but it will not be wasted."

ROOTS

Ten feet beyond the back door
the cottonwood tree
is a steaming stone of beginning time.
A battle-scarred warrior
whose great branches knock
telephone poles aside, mangle trailers
to meager tin-foil in its grasp,
clip chunks of stucco off my house
so sparrows can nest in gaps,
wreck my car hood, splinter
sections of my rail fence,
                all,
                with uncompromising nostalgia
                for warring storms.
I am like this tree
Spanish saddle-makers copied
dressing from.
The dense gray wrath of its bark
is the trackway
shipwrecked captains, shepherds, shepherdesses,
barn-burners, fence cutters followed.
Camped here at the foot of Black Mesa,
beneath this cottonwood,
leaned muskets on this trunk,
stuck knife blades into its canyon valley bark,
red-beaded tasseled arm sleeves clashing
with each throw, as the knife
pierced cattail or bamboo
pinched in bark.

I come back to myself
near this tree, and think of my roots
in this land—

Papa and me working in the field.
I tell Papa, "Look, here comes someone."
He rises, pulls red handkerchief from back pocket,
takes sombrero off, wipes sweat from brow.
You drive up to our field. Unclip briefcase
on the hood of your new government blue car.
Spread official papers out, point with manicured fingers,
telling Papa what he must do.
He lifts a handful of earth by your polished shoe,
and tells you in Spanish, it carries the way of his life.
Before history books were written,
family blood ran through this land,
thrashed against mountain walls and in streams,
fed seeds, and swords, and flowers.
"My heart is a root in this earth!" he said in Spanish, angrily.
You didn't understand Spanish, you told him,
you were not to blame for the way things must be.
The government must have his land.
The Land Grant Deed was no good.
You left a trail of dust in our faces.

I asked Papa how a skinny man like you
could take our land away.
He wept that night, wept a strong cry,
as if blood were pouring from his eyes,
instead of tears. I remember hearing his voice
coming through the walls into my bedroom,
"They twist my arms back and tear the joints,
and they crush my spine with their boots . . ."

In my mind's eye I looked into the man's face
for a long time. I stared at his car for a long time,
and knew as a child I would carry the image
of the enemy in my heart forever.

> Henceforth,
> I will call this cottonwood
> Father.

DREAM INSTRUCTIONS

While in bed, dreams came,
still thinking of the *curandero*'s words,
   ". . . flood of that bull's blood
            will not be wasted. . . ."
I thought of blood wasted, fell asleep, dreams came—

     I appear entering prison.
     Body part of me asleep,
     face cringing, hands tightening,
     terrified,
          saying *no, no, no.* . . .
I am going in,
looking around at bars and walls
     collared with barbwire,
     guard huts.
     Change of shifts,
horrible sounds of guard keys
lifted in a tin bucket on pulley to guard towers,
          rattling
          like a sick man
          with a tube in his throat
          trying to breathe.
I awaken.
Another appears—
     Bearded, on a motorcycle.
     My own voice calls out to him, whistles, wakes me.
     Men I once was want me to return to their skins,
     want me to fill their bodies,
               again.

During afternoon siesta—
     Winged serpent,
     wings warped and scarred
     wrap round its skeleton.
     Wings beat
     blistering hot winds

that sweep desert floor
in search of shade,
then the winged serpent
rests
in the hollow
of a half-buried
petrified skull,
and speaks—

    "Words of love
    would come from my mouth
    if you let them,
    like molten stones shrieking
    from the belly of a volcano.

    Come closer. Come closer.

    But you do not.

    It's been so long now
    since you left.
    Did you tell them
    Hell is not a dream
    and that you've been there,
    did you tell them?"

(Is it the peaceful man
speaking to the destructive one in me?)
I awaken.
Hands pale, fingers cold.

And then the last dream—

I take a deep breath,
dive through my flesh,
past the bone's porous depths,
      a pearl diver

with knife flashing in my teeth,
and come to my heart.
Red throbbing fish
I cut open
and find—

      a great sun, larger than all the mountains,
      glowing,
      and a tapering white horn of ivory,
      twisted by currents of thousands of years' knowledge
      to a perfect taper,
      and a man the size of a sand grain
      sliding down the horn,
      and I see men made of cobwebs,
      standing in line—hair, clothing, and flesh
      rotted away
      so cobwebs cover their standing skeletons,
      and beyond them, endless stretch of darkness,
      eternity of airy darkness,
      and at the far end, all by itself,

      small sparkling bead of light,
      where another way of life thrives.

JAGUAR HEAD

Healed enough months later,
I jump doghouse,
clutch bathroom vent pipe
and pull myself on flat roof
                of my adobe house.
Hoist hand-ax, tar bucket and trowel
with rope tied to my jean's
belt loop.

Early snow fell last night,
cracked a huge cottonwood branch,
that white-sparkled the corners
of my dream, and as I thawed
from dream to reality
                in a bright haze
I dashed out of bed
into the kids' room,
thinking bunkbeds had collapsed.
The house still shuddered from
the branch's thud.

                They were asleep.

Barefoot in boots, wrapped in a bathrobe,
I went outside, swept flashlight
through snow-smoking limbs
and found the snap—
           an immense jaguar head
           snarling busted bark
           and drooling sap
           from fresh-timber fangs.

This morning
I rake its molted fur
of leaves and branches
from rooftop.

LEAPS

Carrots, rice and lamb ribs
on the stove
steam the windows.
Cold and dark outside,
we should be inside.
Instead, chilled cold, noses running,
dirt-smudged faces,
I push my son on his small swing.
In the dark my neighbor's voice
baas, baaing
an ewe into the birthing shed.
In the morning
another mussy-haired lamb
will tremble in the straw,
Mr. Abaskin standing before it,
gray-haired prophet in overalls,
holding kerosene lamp up,
in a perfect nativity scene.
Between my son and me,
my wagon and swing have rusted and broken,
names of buildings changed,
streets widened and paved, and empty dirt lots
crusted with new houses.
But scenes from childhood are sealed in me—
in the blue dusty haze a child plays
on the dirt road, shabbily bordered with adobe houses.
My arms thrust my son into the air,
his delightful cry thrilled
as he ejects from the swing and sails
through the air with his longest leap.

DUST-BOWL MEMORY

for Abaskin

My ancient neighbor, Mr. Abaskin,
was born in Russia, roamed Europe,
and when the call came from America,
he boarded ship and came.
Seventy years farming this land.
Every morning he walks the dirt road
with his aging wife, reminding me
of two solitary mesquite trees
rooted high at the edge of a rocky cliff,
overlooking a vast canyon gorge.
Hands hardened, yellow claws
from farming tenderly pocket candy
in my son's pants.
He scolds his shepherd Kiki
for exciting grazing sheep or scaring
Rhode Island Reds. We meet every noon
by the fence where our feed is
and small talk
conditions of fields,
how he and his wife could buck
three hundred bales an afternoon
when they were my age.
His memory an old dust-bowl town,
he remembers who lived where
before we came, who was born to whom,
when Williams' Packing Company started
stealing people's cattle, when people
started locking their screen doors,
and a time when only Spanish was spoken in this valley.
"Didn't have to go to town. These Mexican folk
had the finest gardens in the world,
why tomatoes and chile you wouldn't believe. . . ."

DAY'S BLOOD

I toss yesterday's tortillas
to pack dogs at my door—
with bared fangs and smoldering
matted scruff-fur hackles,
they grunt-scarf then slouch away.
Snouts in weeds for more chance scraps,
in mournful whines and whimpers, heel-nipping,
with floppy, sagging, lopsided shuffle,
they cross fields towards the Oñate Feedmill,
where they gnaw hooves and snarl
over gutted intestines
at the back door of the slaughter house.
At night they sleep in the Río Grande bosque,
and walking there myself at night,
in the moonlight,
I've seen their eyes glint in the brush,
bloody obsidian knife blades
dripping with the day's blood.

DRAWING LIGHT

Ill-tempered loafer
winter is,
clumps down Black Mesa volcanic rock
with bandaged feet,
his breath icy chimes
stringing my fence wire and tree branches
with bright drippings of notes.
I sling hay slices
over the fence
to horse and cattle huddled by trough.
Hooves lumber in slush,
they chortle steam and grunt chomp into the
hay, flick tails agreeably,
and ogle me—my eyes
draw a kindness out of theirs,
the way darkness
draws its light from falling snowflakes.

THE OTHER SIDE OF THE MOUNTAIN

Distant to friends'
telephone calls, with a nod gruff
I answer
to be left alone. I feel aloof
from everyone.
Over the brittle, haggard fields
wintry silence
opens its eye,
               then closes it.
There is snow on the Sandia mountain peaks.
I think of my old Studebaker
station wagon, breaking down, mid-December.
In my t-shirt, sixteen years old,
I walked in hail and rain,
and an hour later sat under the Placita's underpass,
out of the snow. An old wino next to me said,
               "I'm a farmhand. End of month
               get paid, go into Albuquerque,
               drink and fight.
               My brother at the furniture factory
               gets minimum wage, paid by week,
               and gone by Monday.
               I used to dream what was on the other side
               of the mountain, but every weekend,
               I get drunk, knifed, broken up,
               foot it to where I'm going,
               and curse myself for having my life.
               I follow the crops, all along
               the Río Abajo, and like a leaf, I come
               back, to the old antiques, lamps, chairs,
               jars they sell here in Bernalillo,
               to faces more scarred than I remember them.

               Can't hide my life from others here.
               Used to be good in baseball, math,

then I became a janitor, a little
construction work, then had six kids,
a run-down shack and a mean woman.
I lost my fascination. Almost as if
once you lived here, you feel you know
all there is to know.

Stranger married my sister and she
wouldn't leave. Both of them work
in the furniture factory, owned

by two rich families. Perez and King.
They own everything.
I hope to get enough money to leave
this town, find out maybe, someday,
what's on the other side of the mountain."

After the snow ended, I started walking,
thinking, Nature was not all that cruel.

INTO DEATH BRAVELY

Winter
throws his great white shield
on the ground,
breaking thin arms of twisting branches,
and then howls
on the north side of the Black Mesa
a deep, throaty laughter.
Because of him
we have to sell our cattle
that rake snow for stubble.
Having lived his whole life
in a few weeks,
slow and pensive he walks away,
dragging his silver-stream shield
down branches
and over the ground,
he keeps walking slowly away
into death
bravely.

(HITCHHIKER)

Driving home tonight
I see a hitchhiker
at the end of town.
He sits on a lifetime
packed into his suitcase,
arm extended, thumb pointing south,
toward Mexico.
Where brazen glare of highway lights
ends, and I-40 continues on into endless
prairie, his life unravels
in wind I create as I pass,
a loose thread in darkness,
bit off from the rest, offering
frightening acts or accidental gifts.
Headlights spray across
fleeting outline of his figure—
      a loneliness
in the large black buttons of his overcoat,
      a homelessness
in the leather straps of his English suitcase,
      hard black coldness of coal
in his boots and a sad wisdom in his unshaven face.
He is the pupil
who has stayed after school
the rest of his life,
to write *loneliness* and *love*
on the darkness,
with the chalky pumice of his heart.

KNOWING THE SNOW ANOTHER WAY

Last snowfall of winter.
                I stand at the window
watching, thinking how I have always compared
the White Man to snow.
                   As a child, watching
its graceful fall, my chin
and chest next to a wooden sill, a frost chill
numbed my nose. Each snowflake swirling in space,
making trees gentle ghosts against the night sky
crowding together, and the moon a bonfire
they warmed themselves under,
extending white withered hands and hoary faces
like a religious sect, singing to the moon. . . .

Snow can be pleasing for a child
with no home or family: it means all that never was,
that whatever you do is imprinted,
it is a soothing voice that understands the scars
and covers the ugly sights
with a frill of happiness, light and glittering.
The closest example of the child's heart
is that of a sparrow bathing itself in the morning snow,
scattering the bits into air, speckling bright in sunshine.
But then something happens: at first,
the snow is like those loose sleeves of a prophet
extending its arms to hold a babe, those hollow sleeves
swathe the babe in warmth, and the babe feels the cold
on the cloth collected by the prophet's travels
amongst trees, mountains, streams . . . there is a touch of ice
in the prophet's fingers, of a wilderness
he lives in all alone with his gods.
The child knows this.

And yet, each winter we see what too much snow does.
My own people, trying to obtain Justice and Peace,

are like those people wrecked on a mountain,
wrapped in beggar's clothing, struggling up steep
cliffs. In the frozen faces there is a grim knowledge,
in the moustache sprinkled with snow,
the open eyes and snow-laden eyelashes,
Indios y Chicanos have that stolid death
in their features from knowing the snow's cold, cold extremes.
The dead sheep and cattle, the roads blocked,
no work, the fruits and fields destroyed:
they have known the snow another way, along sidewalks
of any major city, dressed in humble clothing, their breath laboring
against the cold, gritting teeth, blowing on their hands,
standing in soup and employment lines, toes numb
in crusty shoes, in the midst of the storm they exude
a tenderness of loss, their lives like snow
footprints slowly melting.

TOO MUCH OF A GOOD THING

Snow's been melting too soon—
passing the Río Grande every day, I note
water level is high,
all flowing down river.
What happens
when I need to irrigate pastures
in summer
and there is no water?
Farmers get edgy.
Start cursing neighbors under their breath
for using too much water.
Crops stunted,
only one alfalfa cutting
instead of three,
no feed for cows,
no money to buy feed . . .
and then like it happened a few years ago,
Mr. Gonzales goes out
and you hear rifle shots blister
cold morning air,
and you know his cattle
are falling in snow,
dead.
At Coronado Center, biggest shopping mall
in New Mexico, I hear two suntanned ladies
praising our wonderful weather. I give them
a glance, throw my gloves
on the counter for the cashier, and wonder what
a farmer's wife would tell them.

KNOWING WHEN

Sun buries its face
in dark brown
landscape of the West Mesa.

Woman I love
buries my chin
in her breast with pleasure,

teaches me,
to have a good spring,
I need a good winter.

BIRTHING WORK

Adobe brick.
Mix sand and water as mortar,
palm it on, lay adobe down,
smooth out overlapping mud,
let dry smooth.
Simplicity of this type of building
becomes music, I scratch-rub
out designs (sun, snake, my own second-name sign),
nichos for *santos, horno* to keep pan warm.
I stand back after days of work
to appraise my sculpture,
Rilke in front of his Grecian statue—
I will cook in here, sleep in here,
stare outside at others staring in,
I am a seed crouched in my work,
shaken free from my heart's green vine,
to blossom the doorway,
a wall, an indoor spring.
Drowsy sleep that absorbs dormant fields
this time of year absorbs me.
I hose off mud from face and arms,
and in my head see an image
of a newborn child washed off by midwife,
blood mud toweled, warm wash cloth
to its small body,
I let water run down my arms
glistening bushy forearm hair
of the babe's head.

Adobes I didn't use
I toss into the old truck.
Stack of dried hearts
cut out of the riverbed
had grown weeds.

Round and rough
hearts of old warriors
wind will wild weed again,
sun warm and nurture
back into earth.
My heart will go like this.

PRAISE

From Isleta Pueblo church
evening mass bells bellow.
Trembling gray wheat stubble,
thrashing brittle bamboo and cattails,
crackling pasture grass,
the notes trample, up Black Mesa,
down Black Mesa, great horses
dragging boulders away, their breath
the sunset that explodes
red cloud dust on the West Mesa.

Blackbirds
sing from tattered hymn books
of cottonwood branches.
Beneath them I gaze up
to their ancient altar of wood,
black-robed monks
faithful, making a pure offering of love
to the light, in one great orchestrated
lift their wings beat a black cloud
that glides over fields, spirals and swoops,
incense from an earth censor
swung by an altar boy, smoke of their flight
fills church the field is.

BELLS

Bells. The word gongs my skull bone. . . .
Mamá carried me out, just born,
swaddled in hospital blanket,
from St. Vincent's in Santa Fe.
Into the evening, still drowsed
with uterine darkness,
my fingertips purple with new life,
cathedral bells splashed
into my blood, plunging iron hulls
into my pulse waves. Cathedral steeples,
amplified brooding, sonorous bells,
through narrow cobbled streets, bricked patios,
rose trellis'd windows,
red-tiled Spanish rooftops, bells
beat my name, "Santiago! Santiago!"
Burning my name in black-frosted streets,
bell sounds curved and gonged deep,
ungiving, full-bellowed beats of iron on iron,
shuddering pavement Mamá walked,
quivering thick stainless panes, creaking
plaza shop doors, beating its gruff thuds
down alleys and dirt
passageways, past men waiting in doorways
of strange houses. Mamá carried me, past
peacocks and chickens, past the miraculous
stairwell winding into the choirloft, touted
in tourist brochures, *"Not one nail was used
to build this, it clings tenaciously
together by pure prayer power, a spiraling
pinnacle of faith. . . ."* And years later,
when I would do something wrong,
in kind reprimand Mamá would say,
"You were born of bells, more than my womb,

they speak to you in dreams.
Ay, *Mejito,*
you are such a dreamer!"

A GOD LOOSENED

I walk along the *acequía*.
Morning quivers softly.
Glassy sunlight sparkles
in the yellowed grass.
Sparrow flicks from a tree
across marginless blue sky.
        All that drips,
glows, hollows a bright flash
out of the morning.
A flickering chill
blows and uplifts flame
of this day brighter.

In the upturned claws
of great dead eagles
that are the snowy woods
along the Río Grande,
echoes a crumbling and falling
of icy sounds,
of logs and trunks cracking
in a crackling crush of dead leaves.
The wings of a hawk storm
from tangled boughs, wings woop fiercely
in above-ground canyons of branches,
drumming the air,
and in the frightful break of silence,
suddenly, it seems a God has loosened
itself in those terrible feathers.

MAIN CHARACTER

I went to see
How The West Was Won
at the Sunshine Theater.
Five years old,
deep in a plush seat,
light turned off,
bright screen lit up
with MGM roaring lion—
>   in front of me
>   a drunk Indian rose,
>   cursed
>   the western violins
>   and hurled his uncapped bagged bottle
>   of wine
>   at the rocket roaring to the moon.

His dark angry body
convulsed with his obscene gestures
at the screen,
and then ushers escorted him
up the aisle,
and as he staggered past me,
I heard his grieving sobs.
>   Red wine streaked
>   blue sky and take-off smoke,
>   sizzled cowboys' campfires,
>   dripped down barbwire,
>   slogged the brave, daring scouts
>   who galloped off to mesa buttes
>   to speak peace with Apaches,
>   and made the prairie
>   lush with wine streams.

When the movie
was over,

I squinted at the bright
sunny street outside,
looking for the main character.

AS CHILDREN KNOW

Elm branches radiate green heat,
blackbirds stiffly strut across fields.
Beneath bedroom wood floor, I feel earth—
bread in an oven that slowly swells,
simmering my Navajo blanket thread-crust
as white-feathered and corn-tasseled
Corn Dancers rise in a line, follow my calf,
vanish in a rumple and surface at my knee-cliff,
chanting. Wearing shagged buffalo headgear,
Buffalo Dancer chases Deer Woman across
Sleeping Leg mountain. Branches of wild rose
trees rattle seeds. Deer Woman fades into hills
of beige background. Red Bird
of my heart thrashes wildly after her.
What a stupid man I have been!
How good to let imagination go,
step over worrisome events,
                    those hacked logs
                    tumbled about
                    in the driveway.
Let decisions go!
                    Let them blow
                    like school children's papers
                    against the fence,
                    rattling in the afternoon wind.
This Red Bird
of my heart thrashes within the tidy appearance
I offer the world,
topples what I erect, snares what I set free,
dashes what I've put together,
indulges in things left unfinished,
and my world is left, as children know,
                    left as toys after dark in the sandbox.

SPRING

       With one mighty tug and push, conservancy engineers
in Northern New Mexico
       open water gates—snow-melt,
brimming northern lakes, and streams
       gush, lunge, and hurl down Río Abajo to community fields,
       fill the dry ditches and canals, clashing
like great banging orchestra cymbals
against dirt. Plants, bushes, weeds
       uncurl, furl out along my ditch,
       ants float on islands of leaves,
       past pyramids of beer cans,
       tadpoles fuse to the water
       in swirls of brown mist,
       catfish fin beneath driftwood
       and stew the water dark brown.
All things pull and strain. The ditch swells
into a great marketplace, where death and life
are exchanged.
A pair of light blue-grey doves skim water surface,
geese veer down, royal couriers
flap-landing in gusty sprinkles, then
serenely floating like white flags of peace,
drifting in pairs, through glare and shadows,
       as crawdads, spiders, snakes and frogs
       peer from mud and weed corners.

From each unfolding lilac leaf
a blue-green arctic haze glimmers,
from feathers dark winter melts,
from eyes glide out cold deeps,
everything bears a new light.
The crane is breaking ice with its call,
long-legged spider skitters
to birth-thawing rhythms of the shore,

as spring finally arrives,
glistening the dead-slag of winter
in all creatures,
as they emit that special light
they do.

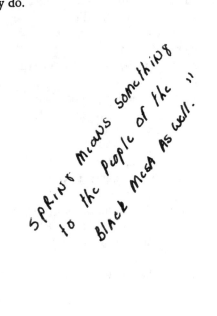

" spring means something
to the people of the "
to the people of the "
black mesa as well.

AT NIGHT

I lie in bed
and hear the soft throb of water
surging through the ditch,
from extreme to extreme water bounds,
clumsy country boy,
stumbling over fallen logs and rubber tires
to meet a lover
who awaits in her parents' house, window open.

As I used to for love.

Now gray-black hair,
vigorous cheeks, weathered brow, chapped lips,
dismal thoughtful eyes,
I float in brown melancholy on the lazy currents
of memory, studying my reflection
on the water this night,
with distant devotion,
a swimmer who has forgotten how to swim.

GOD'S COMING

I await the burning books
of lilac buds
to flame. This year I promise myself
to read them
as they are opening
before they burn away.
Along the front of my house
silent tombs of lilac bushes
await God's coming,
rising out of each bud
fleshed with petals.
Now, He grafts Himself
to dirt, piecing Himself together
a worm.

MATANZA TO WELCOME SPRING

for Pat and Victorio

Spread eagle sheep legs wide,
wire hooves to shed beams,
and sink blade in neck wool,
'til the gray eyes drain of life
like cold pure water
from a tin pail.

> (It kicked, choking on nasal blood,
> liquid gasping coughs
> spattered blood over me.)

Slit down belly, scalp rug-wool
skin away, pinch wool back
with blade to pink flesh, ssst ssst ssst
inch by inch, then I sling
whole carcass in bloody spray over fence.

> (Close to its face, I swear
> it gift-heaved a last breath
> from its soft black nose
> and warmed my nostril hairs
> as I sniffed the dark smell
> of its death.)

Mesquite in hole
boils water in the iron cauldron
which steam-cooks
hind quarter
on grill across cauldron.

> Tonight I invite men and women
> *con duende,*
> who take a night in life
> and forge it into iron
> in the fire of their vision.

Aragon has gone
to the river to play his drum.

I hear the deep pom pom pom.
Round bonfire
Alicia squats, ruffles sheaf of poems,
while Alejandro tunes guitar.
Shadows dance round
stones that edge the fire.
                    (In Alejandro's boot
                    a knife hilt glimmers.)
Their teeth gleam grease juice
                    (as do those of the children, who play
                    in the dark behind us).
There is fear
in the horse's eye
corralled nearby.
                    (Hear the drum on the Río Grande.
                    Boom pom boom pom. . . .)
Blood sizzles,
moist alfalfa in the air,
bats flit above the flames.
I toss a gleaming bone to spirits
in the orchard,
and Gonzales yells,
with his old earthen voice,
"Play, *hombre, ¡Canta, mujer!* Sing!
Sing the way the old ones sang!"

        Tonight life is
        lust
        death
        hunger
        violence
        innocence
        sweetness
        honor
        hard work
        and tomorrow I will go
        to church.

But tonight
I leap into
impulse, instinct,
into the burning
of
       this moment.

      (I commit myself! One moment to the next
I am chasm jumper and silence is
a blue fire on my papery soul. I construct
out of nothing. I am air, am labyrinth,
place with no entry or exit,
am a smoking mirror.

Commit myself! Storms stroke my heart
and destroy its neat furrows.
My words are mule teams,
that loosen, pound, hurl, out and up,
and leave me standing in the open, naked,
with star flame roar, life opening. . . .

      Commit myself!)

Hear the two hands
bleed along the river beating
drumskins,
deep sounds of thu-uba,
of magic, despair, joy,
      emotions trance-weave through sound,
           thumba, thumba, thumba.
Follow drum,
      thumba thumba thumba,
      umba umba umba
      ba-ba ba-ba
      thumba thumba thumba,
hear hearts mate with earth

in song,
spiral toward death

        in its long thuuumbaa,
toward life again
    in ba-ba ba-ba.

The sound is stain on purity,
is cry of broken thing,
drum does not wither beneath bed,
but rises heart
      into newness around us,
all around us,
      come follow   Follow the drum,
      thumba thumba thumba
           ba—ba—ba
      thumba thumba thumba
           ba—ba—ba,

      of living!

LLANO VAQUEROS

Padilla unloads mangy herd of Mexican
cattle in the field.
Meaner, horns long and sharp
for bloody battle, lean from a diet
of prairie weed, looking more
like cattle did years ago
on the plains
than cattle now—
sluggish, pampered globs
stalled year round
for State Fair Judges to admire,
stall-salon dolls, hooves manicured
and polished, hide-hair blow-dried, lips
and lashes waxed.
I ride down the dirt road
on Sunshine (my bay mare)
and she smarts
away from their disdainful glare—
come in, try to lasso us,
try to comb our hair.
I admire my ancestors, *llano vaqueros,*
who flicked a home-made cigarette in dust,
spit in scuffed gloves, grabbed one
by the horns, wrestled it down,
branded it, with the same pleasure
they enjoyed in a bunk-house brawl.

GREEN CHILE

I prefer red chile over my eggs
and potatoes for breakfast.
Red chile *ristras* decorate my door,
dry on my roof, and hang from eaves.
They lend open-air vegetable stands
historical grandeur, and gently swing
with an air of festive welcome.
I can hear them talking in the wind,
haggard, yellowing, crisp, rasping
tongues of old men, licking the breeze.

        But grandmother loves green chile.
When I visit her,
she holds the green chile pepper
in her wrinkled hands.
Ah, voluptuous, masculine,
an air of authority and youth simmers
from its swan-neck stem, tapering to a flowery
collar, fermenting resinous spice.
A well-dressed gentleman at the door
my grandmother takes sensuously in her hand,
rubbing its firm glossed sides,
caressing the oily rubbery serpent,
with mouth-watering fulfillment,
fondling its curves with gentle fingers.
Its bearing magnificent and taut
as flanks of a tiger in mid-leap,
she thrusts her blade into
and cuts it open, with lust
on her hot mouth, sweating over the stove,
bandanna round her forehead,
mysterious passion on her face
as she serves me green chile con carne
between soft warm leaves of corn tortillas,

with beans and rice—her sacrifice
to her little prince.
I slurp from my plate
with last bit of tortilla, my mouth burns
and I hiss and drink a tall glass of cold water.

All over New Mexico, sunburned men and women
drive rickety trucks stuffed with gunny-sacks
of green chile, from Belen, Veguita, Willard, Estancia,
San Antonio y Socorro, from fields
to roadside stands, you see them roasting green chile
in screen-sided homemade barrels, and for a dollar a bag,
we relive this old, beautiful ritual again and again.

SWEET REVENGE

Kirtland Airforce jets
fly over my house, scorch air
with ear-deafening screams
of gnashing war-teeth.
In kitchens and yards
people stop talking
when they fly overhead,
then resume conversations.
They fly so low,
sometimes I see pilot's black helmet.
I can't hear my voice curse them,
as I see my infant's mouth contort
in terror as his cradle rattles.
Driving my wife to work
one evening, up Gibson, I read
a bumper sticker—

Jet Noise, The Sound of Freedom

I speed up
side by side to the driver
in a blue Airforce suit,
who never saw a finger
flying with such relish
as I flipped at him.

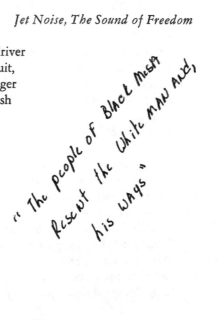

" The people of Black Mesa
resent the White man and,
his ways "

A GOOD DAY

Saturday.
Freckled leaves after rain,
water pools sprinkled like paw prints
over the road.
                    With bare feet
                    my heart dips
                    into the rainbow
                    by the red cloud.
My dog
shakes water from his fur,
I shiver with wild joy!

I rise,
swing my porch door open
to break the intolerable calm
between myself and the poem
I am working on.
A robin swirls
haltingly into the screenless door,
wings frantically beating
backflight at seeing me,
as my own soul does
at seeing itself
before the blank paper.

A check arrived in the afternoon mail.
To celebrate, we go to a second-hand store
and buy a lime-green patio set.
On the front porch,
beneath the green/white striped Italian umbrella,
Beatrice and I sip cappuccino.
Our Irish setter Kianne
slumps in the unmown front yard grass, auburn
lump of burred rug, nip-teasing

a dead black duck
dragged in from fields across the road.
Light that left stars millions of years ago
reaches us now
and blesses my brow.

WHAT WE DON'T TELL THE CHILDREN

Feathers in the yard this morning.
My cat?
Or the two black strays,
ominously staring with orange eyes
from corrugated, rusted sheep-shed roof?
I hear them at night
yeowling—
shush of branches, squeals and shrieks,
then silence.

Tufts of rabbit fur
in backfield weeds, shred of meat
still warm on bones,
blood drops in warm earth.

Artist couple rented around the
corner last month. Were ecstatic
about this *primitive place.*
She came over one morning,
arm bandaged, boyfriend
stern-faced, sucking air through teeth,
she said, "My cat went belly up,
no animal is supposed to attack another
belly up. Those blacks are vicious.
Ought to be put to sleep."
Her Siamese crossed Blacks' territory,
she came upon them, kicked one Black,
and it scratched her arm in defense.

They moved out month after they moved in,
truck loaded with paintbrushes, canvasses,
cameras, to find another *primitive place*
near Santa Fe, quaint artistic place,
tranquil as a pond in autumn evening

where golden-tipped wheat leans,
place with no problems, no animal
attacks another, where gentle folk
are as groomed as heirloom porcelain,
where there is no pollution, no drugs,
no world gone belly-up
the rest of us are trying to heal.

After they left, Antonio and I
sat on the patio, talking how he
and Blacks played hide-n-seek,
how he crouched in cool cracks
reaching his arm under boards
by the fence, they squirmed under,
pawing at him playfully, their claws
tucked in their furry mitten-paws
safely.
"Where's the other Black Papi?"

"I don't know, *mejito*," I said.

WHAT'S REAL AND WHAT'S NOT

Bob greases himself up
in his garage,
works on his Volkswagen bus,
away from wife and kids for a while,
smells of oily work table,
exhaust and oil, he grunts a valve
to millimeter perfection, purrs
timing screw to a coaxing rrrrr rrrr—
saving money by doing
his own work.
Helping me
with my Volkswagen, he looks up,
oil-smudged face, greasy-handed, nostrils
black, and says,
                  "This is real Jim. Feel that energy"—
                  He revs it. "Runs better.
                  Beats paying two hundred
                  dollars, when we can do it ourselves."
It's real.

Following week
Bob and I go camping.
(Confident of his work, and proud,
he wants to try Doris,
as he calls his van, on steep mountain terrain.)

My singleness glimmers bright,
and my first time from home in months
makes the land glow, the sky bluer,
and the asphalt road
winding to the foothills
ignites each nerve into a sacred torch.

An ex-vet Nam grunt,
instead of going back to New York,

Bob became a back-packing
stick-handed hillman,
herding goat flocks in Placitas,
with ram-wool beard waist long,
he roamed gopher-warted *arroyos*,
up snake-burrowed coyote trails,
healing himself in shady cedar groves
and yucca patches.

We snuggle in our sleeping bags,
look up at stars,
and want our lives to be simple
flames of natural blue gas
rising from ground hills,
plentiful, innocent
from the bowels of earth.
From his bag, Bob stares into the dark sky,
atop Sandia Crest, at radio transmission poles
blink red lights of flying mortar.

Second night set camp, and at midnight
follow boulder bottom trail
full moon fevering in its folds, heel-skid
from graveled crust to smooth
stream gulley silt,
and follow roadside stream up.

Suddenly, Bob plunges
into creekside brush,
splash-wading stream,
belly-down
over bloated bodies
with dead-leaf eyes,
then he sloshes up
bloody banks, amid dying coughs. . . .

and springs out
of the brush as quickly,

sopping wet, shivering
red-faced in full Cambodian moon,
old exhilaration of Nam patrol
in pin-blue eyes.

I show him
the old preacher's rock house
clothed in a century of wild clover
and thorned laurel,
caved-in ceiling *vigas*
charred by livestock rubbings and dung,
herded here
during bad winter storms.

On the way back to Burque next morning,
we passed Willard, Estancia, Moriarty,
towns hollowed by decades of blowing prairie dust.

Stones here are dream rooms
with answers to my questions.
Those I know from various pueblos,
their lives are white cloaks
my words wear on freezing nights.
Black hounds of Bob's tires
bound us toward the dark, hostile angels
of the city, panting *necessity! necessity!*
over cattle guards and *arroyo* dips,
tearing up the delicate blue stems
of hours we spent camping.

We enter city limits,
and the torch my body is
dims to old darkness again.

OLD WOMAN

I see Señora Sanchez
along the river.
Black catfish
pop the silver
water surface,
waves unroll
as the gnarled
bronze face and
black eyes
remember
cool sea shells
and warm turquoise,
the turkey gobbling
behind bushes,
and the red skirt
hanging on boughs
as she bathed. . . .
She pulls her black sweater
snug around her, folded arms
across her stomach.
She who remembers
cannot say amen
but smiles to sunrise
as she walks through the grass,
                        the tall,
                            green grass,
grass that does not listen to
                        the priest
in black robes, blooms green
as she walks through the grass
and talks with them.

WISHES

As spring ends today, this morning
I hope to find an angel
in the kitchen,
who would ask, "How can I help?"

Those men in the Bible
barefoot down dirt roads,
encountered glowing angels
whose counsel dulled their hunger
and blinded their sinful eyes.

        I would like some bills paid,
        maybe a small vacation
        hundred miles from here,
        new clothing for all of us.

Wry smile
to myself
as I make coffee,
breakfast for the kids,
empty garbage
and sweep kitchen.

        I glance round the kitchen
        into the air
        for a sign.   No.

My sons appear
from under the kitchen table.
They smell of freshly rinsed
vegetable greens
as I dress them.
Their giggling laughter
scatters

in a shower of gold flecks over the air
that settles in the wake of their wings
onto the kitchen floor,
as they run out the screen door to play.

CHOICES

An acquaintance at Los Alamos Labs
who engineers weapons
black x'd a mark where I live
on his office map.
Star-wars humor. . . .
He exchanged muddy boots
and patched jeans
for a white intern's coat
and black polished shoes.
A month ago, after butchering a gouged bull,
we stood on a pasture hill,
and he wondered with pained features
where money would come from
to finish his shed, plant alfalfa,
and fix his tractor.
Now his fingers
yank horsetail grass,
he crimps herringbone tail-seed
between teeth, and grits out words,
"Om gonna buy another tractor
next week. More land too."
Silence between us is gray water
let down in a tin pail
in a deep, deep well,
a silence
milled in continental grindings
millions of years ago.
I throw my heart
into the well, and it falls
a shimmering pebble to the bottom.
Words are hard
to come by. "Would have lost everything
I've worked for, not takin' the job."

His words try to
retrieve
my heart
from the deep well.
We walk on in silence,
our friendship
rippling away.

FAMILY TIES

Mountain barbecue.
They arrive, young cousins singly,
older aunts and uncle in twos and threes,
like trees. I play with a new generation
of children, my hands in streambed silt
of their lives, a scuba diver's hands, dusting
surface sand for buried treasure.
Freshly shaved and powdered faces
of uncles and aunts surround taco
and tamale tables. Mounted elk head on wall,
brass rearing horse cowboy clock
on fireplace mantle. Sons and daughters
converse round beer and whiskey table.
Tempers ignite on land grant issues.
Children scurry round my legs.
Old bow-legged men toss horseshoes on lawn,
other farmhands from Mexico sit on a bench,
broken lives repaired for this occasion.
I feel no love or family tie here. I rise
to go hiking, to find abandoned rock cabins
in the mountains. We come to a grass clearing,
my wife rolls her jeans up past ankles,
wades ice cold stream, and I barefooted,
carry a son in each arm and follow.
We cannot afford a place like this.
At the party again, I eat bean and chile
burrito, and after my third glass of rum,
we climb in the car and my wife drives
us home. My sons sleep in the back,
dream of the open clearing,
they are chasing each other with cattails
in the sunlit pasture, giggling,
as I stare out the window
at no trespassing signs white flashing past.

PICKING PIÑONS

On my knees
beneath piñon tree,
I sift shellwood petals
in black grainy dirt chips that
inscribe on my finger tips a time
when earth made hands
bleed and crack
and gave meaning to our pain.

        Throw my coat on the ground
        and shake the tree.
Palm piñons in my coffee can,
then knock pocketknife
handle against stubborn acorns
fringed with thawing ochre.
And the brown-shelled dreamers
softly drop
into my can held aloft beneath each cone—

        My hand goes to catch a piñon
        and
        I feel a murmur in the tree's
        tongue
        against my bare arm
        telling of a stable world.

As it gets dark,
I sit on a boulder
and scan the valley below.
Hidden rock hollows
are rooms
where wind is a small boy
who practices piano,
fingering key after key for a missing note.

The boy plays a melody
of a one-legged man,
one-armed man,
one-eyed man.

One,
all alone in my imbalance.

WORK WE HATE AND DREAMS WE LOVE

Every morning
Meiyo revs his truck up
and lets it idle. Inside the small adobe house,
he sips coffee
while his Isleta girlfriend
Cristi
brownbags his lunch.
Life is filled with work
Meiyo hates,
and while he saws, 2 × 4's,
trims lengths of 2 × 10's on table saw,
inside his veins another world
in full color etches
a blue sky on his bones,
a man following a bison herd,
and suddenly his hammer becomes a spear
he tosses to the ground
uttering a sound we do not understand.

ACCOUNTABILITY

Who we are and what we do
appears to us
like a man dressed in a long black coat,
a bill collector
who offers a paper to sign
and says we have no choice
but to sign it.
In it,
we read who we are—
we should change this paragraph,
or the color of the hair,
or the time we took a trip,
or the woman we met in a coffeeshop,
it's not true,
or it didn't turn out quite that way.
"Sign it,"
he says,
"I have many others to see today."

PERFECTO FLORES

for Perfecto

We banter
back and forth
the price
for laying brick.
"You people only pay
the rich, those who
already have money.
I have a whole yard of bricks
collected over thirty years
working as a mason.
I offer you a good price,
load them on the truck,
bring sand and gravel,
do the work almost for nothing,
and you won't pay me
half what Hunter charges."
He was right, I relented,
paid him seventy cents a block.
The next day
he brought them,
towing cement mixer
behind his old truck.
He rounded the weeping willow
trunk with blocks
left over from apartments
he worked on
six years ago,
then poured cement
and troweled it smooth.
After he was done, he asked,
"Can I have that roll of wire back there?"
He lives my scraps, built three houses
for his daughters with construction site

scraps.
In English
his name is Perfect Flower.
Brawny man with bull shoulders,
who forty years ago came from Mexico,
tired of the mines, the somnolent
spirit of Mexicans. ". . . I was the first one
to say I wouldn't ride the old bus.
It was falling apart. I refused, and
the rest followed, and soon a new bus
was brought up the mountain."
I gave him our old Falcon
for pouring cement floor
in the guest cottage,
jar of blessed black-purple
Acoma corn kernels
for helping me uproot a tree,
gave him seven rabbits
and a box of chickens
for helping me cut adobe arches.
We curse and laugh as we work.
He proudly hefts a wheelbarrow
brimmed with cement. "Ah! Sixty-two, *cabrón!*
And you, naa! You would break your back!"
He ribs me, proud of his strength.
He has nothing that glows his face
so much as stories of his working years,
feats of courage in the mines
when he was called upon to defuse dynamite
that didn't explode. Short, stocky
gray-haired man, always in his yard
scattering chicken seed, nailing, sawing,
always in jean overalls.
Chews a ground weed,
carries a stub pencil and grimy wad of paper
for figuring, and
always turns to me when I drive

or walk into his yard
with a roguish grin,
his love of telling stories
competing with mine.
He growls with laughter
at the blisters on my hands,
takes his gloves off,
spreads his palms up—
a gallery owner who strips black cloth
off his prized Van Gogh painting,
"Look! You could sharpen a file
on these hands," he grins proudly.

INVASIONS

for Eddie

6:00 a.m.
I awake and leave to fish
the Jemez.
Coronado rode
through this light, dark
green brush,
horse foaming saliva,
tongue red and dry
as the red cliffs.
Back then the air
was bright and crisp
with Esteban's death
at the hands of Zuñi warriors.
Buffalo God, as he was called,
was dead, dead, dead,
beat the drums
and rattled gourds.
The skin of the Moor
was black
as a buffalo's nose,
hair kinky
as buffalo shag-mane.
No seven cities
of Cíbola gold were found.
Horses waded the Jemez,
white frothing currents
banking horse bellies,
beading foot armor,
dripping from sword scabbards.
I wade in
up to my thighs
in jeans,
throw hooked

salmon egg bait
out in shadowy shallows
beneath overhanging cottonwood, and
realize
I am the end result
of Conquistadores,
Black Moors,
American Indians,
and Europeans,
bloods rainbowing
and scintillating
in me
like the trout's flurrying
flank scales
shimmering a fight
as I reel in.
With trout
on my stringer
I walk downstream
toward my truck.
"How'd you do?" I ask
an old man walking past,
          "Caught four—biting pretty good
          down near that elm."
I walk south
like Jemez and Pecos pueblos
during 1690 uprisings,
when Spanish came north
to avenge their dead.
Indians fled
canyon rock shelters,
settling in present day
open plains.
Trout flails like a saber
dangling from scabbard stringer
tied to my belt,
chop-whacking long-haired weeds.

Peace here now. Bones
dissolved, weapons rusted.
I stop, check my sneaker prints
in moist sandy bank.
Good deep marks.
I clamber up an incline,
crouch in bushes
as my ancestors did,
peer at vacation houses
built on rock shelves,
sun decks and travel trailers—
the new invasion.

MI TÍO BACA EL POETA DE SOCORRO

Antonio Ce De Baca
chiseled on stone chunk gravemarker,
propped against a white wooden cross.
Dust storms faded the birth and death numbers.
Poet de Socorro,
whose poems roused *la gente*
to demand their land rights back,
'til one night—that terrible night,
hooves shook your earthen-floor
one-room adobe, lantern flame
flickered shadowy omens on walls,
and you scrawled across the page,
"*¡Aquí vienen! ¡Aquí vienen!*
Here they come!"
Hooves clawed your front yard,
guns glimmering blue
angrily beating at your door.
                          You rose.
Black boots scurried round four adobe walls,
trampling flower beds.
They burst through the door.
It was a warm night, and carried the scent
of their tobacco, sulphur, and leather.
Faces masked in dusty hankies,
men wearing remnants of Rinche uniforms,
arms pitchforked you out,
where arrogant young boys on horses
held torches and shouted,
"Shoot the Mexican! Shoot him!"
Saliva flew from bits
as horses reared from you,
while red-knuckled recruits held reins tight,
drunkenly pouring whiskey over you,
kicking you up the hill by the yucca,

where you turned, and met the scream
of rifles with your silence.

              Your house still stands.
Black burnt tin covers window openings,
weeds grow on the dirt roof
that leans like an old man's hand
on a cane *viga*. . . .
I walk to the church a mile away,
a prayer on my lips bridges
years of disaster between us.
Maybe things will get better.
Maybe our struggle to speak and be
as we are, will come about.
For now, I drink in your spirit, Antonio,
to nourish me as I descend
into dangerous abysses of the future.
I came here this morning
at 4:30 to walk over my history.
Sat by the yucca, and then imagined you again,
walking up to me
face sour with tortuous hooks
pulling your brow down in wrinkles,
cheeks weary with defeat,
face steady with implacable dignity.
The softness in your brown eyes
said you could take no more.
You will speak with the angels now.
I followed behind you to the church,
your great bulky field-working shoulders
lean forward in haste
as if angels really did await us.
Your remorseful footsteps
in crackly weeds
sound the last time
I will hear and see you. Resolve is engraved
in each step. I want to believe

whatever problems we have, time will take
its course, they'll be endured and consumed.
Church slumps on a hill, somber and elegant.
After you, I firmly pull the solid core door back.
You kneel before La Virgen De Guadalupe,
bloody lips moving slightly,
your great gray head poised in listening,
old jacket perforated with bloody bullet holes.
I close the door, and search the prairie,
considering the words *faith, prayer* and *forgiveness,*
wishing, like you, I could believe them.

CHILD OF THE SUN—GABRIEL'S BIRTH (SUN PRAYER)

to Gabriel

Beatrice on the bed, muscles twitch pain,
                    "No, uh, the pain. . . ."
Marsha offers warm wet towel,
                    "No, no, no, it's too painful. . . ."
Beatrice paces bedroom, cross corn-planting blanket,
                    barefoot through rows of Corn Dancers,
caressing abdomen, deep breathing,
lips expelling flurries of pain,
while her fingers circle belly-button,
trying to ease the pain.
                    In a tub of warm water,
                    Beatrice rises,
                    "O, uhh, no," pulls my hands into hers.
We stand together in the bathroom,
window sunlight at her back
silhouettes her body
to a shadow sunlight smolders off of.
She radiates light streams,
her face grimaces intense pain and pleasure,
her head lolls forward, her long black hair
veils my face
as I kneel before her on the bathroom floor, and say,
"Prop your right leg on the toilet seat,
that's it, now push, push, sweetheart. . . ."
Through vines of hair I peer,
between her spread legs, where blinding light
streams through. Our dark bodies
create a cave dwelling, entered through hair.
                    She mutters grunted pleas,
                    aggressive throaty squeals,
                    grips my shoulders,
                    her warm breath pants at my head,
                    her body,

drips sweat onto mine.
Sunlight radiates
through wild roses and green vines
that press against the window
at her back,
and rages between her legs.
       She gives a half-choked sob
       and upside down
       suspended between her legs
       surfacing from sunlight,
       leaves and flowers,
       a thousand-year-old face appears,
       Gabriel! Gabriel!
       Flying dark shape in sunlight,
       God descending from sky
       upside down
       between woman's legs,
       arms and face glisten darkly with uterine juice,
       shimmery,
       it wriggles free of mother skin,
       fierce glum godhead stone face
       I stare at through vine hair,
       its dark eyes squinch-lidded
       unwrinkle wide in haunting ferocity
at me,
and instantly I am tossed,
from my body into a wheel of sunlight,
disembodied
in sheer blaze of dazzling lightwaves,
I am hurled
like a spark from my chimney-flue body
on an updraft of his presence—

       Gabriel slips from her trembling loins,
       filmy with juice,
       thick rivulets of blood
       run down our hands, arms, wrists,

into my hands,
                    cries angrily at me,
and I brush through vines of hair,
rise in blue sunlight haze
misting the bathroom,
and offer Gabriel, child of the Sun,
                    to Beatrice,
then look at the window
and bow to the sunlight,
for our child's safe arrival.

PERSONAL PRAYERS

On a red wagon
we pull the knee-high blue spruce
out of the nursery (plant pound),
tag round its scruffy branch
directing
us when we arrive home
to keep it in the shed for a week.
Week before last harvest moon
we set it on the patio to breathe
in fresh air,
its needles limbering
and wagging happily at the coldness.
On full moon
we brought it in, decorated it,
branches curled with delightful weights
of Kachina dolls, eagle and hawk feathers,
wooden figurines of mothers holding children,
the fireplace
lapping motherly warmth
over its spiny branches.

After full moon I dug a hole on the north side
of the house,
emptied two buckets of black vegetable mulch,
kneaded in dry horse manure,
and finger-crunched dug-up dirt
fine.
From a plastic bread bag
in the freezer, I took out Gabriel's placenta,
rinsed it under hot tap water.
With blood-reddened hands,
I dropped the placenta in the hole,
shoveled in soil, manure and mulch,
dumped the blue spruce from black planter bucket

into the hole, and gently tapped soil firm
with heel of my boot and shovel handle.
Then bending an inch from the soil,
I whispered,

> "Mother earth, give my son deep
> strong roots. Care for him
> throughout his life, give him
> a path filled with light, give him
> the courage to bear himself
> upright, as corn, as this spruce tree
> gift I offer you in thankfulness,
> Mother earth."

SINCE YOU'VE COME

for Antonio

You make
a thousand expressions of distaste
and indifference, like a bored prince
unimpressed with our performance,
you scream
and we stagger out of bed,
grumbling at the unmerciful rule
of our emperor.
We become fortune-tellers
guessing what you desire.
We become dwarfs
at your service,
jugglers of toy bears and rattlers,
musicians continually winding up the music box,
and after all of it, you simply
shut your eyes, burp, and go to sleep.
We have never loved anyone more than you
my child.

WHAT COULD HAVE BEEN AND WHAT IS

for Bea

Beatrice nurses Gabriel.
He muzzles the brown flower at her breast
in cotton folds of her blouse
soft as leafy alfalfa.
First few minutes of his life
he was the color of blue corn.
Beatrice glances up at me, smiles—
in her lingering glance an old sadness
floats between us.
Had I not become a poet,
I would have been a bandit in the mountains,
her eyes say. Had I not,
I would be sitting on the West Mesa
swigging pints of El Presidente,
shattering empty rum bottles in my hands
as I keep beat with
Alejandro strumming his guitar,
touching the dark frets of wounds in me,
and turning to music the anger, shame, pain in my life.
Her brown eyes and the lingering look
have a clean, brilliant laboring glow
of raising a family, of being loyal and honest,
loving a man in constant struggle with himself,
who sometimes walked through the door
on mornings, unshaven and uncombed for days,
unable to speak his joy or suffering.
Under the weeping willow,
on the cement bench built round its trunk,
between swaying weeping willow branches,
we glance at each other—
an after-storm calm look,
after red landscapes of the heart
have earthquaked,

and we
have avalanched our seismic freedoms
and created our own terrains
of our lives, and the ravenous molten furies
of our words have cooled to
clear, placid streams,
we cup water in our palms from
and drink—
        we who broke into a million
        cleavages of terror
        like a diamond,
        in a heat flash of hot nights
        and shimmering dawns,
        fused to each other
        in our darkest moments,
        and made ourselves
        new stars.

Gabriel is the faint light of daybreak
in the cloudy folds of her blouse.
The sun sets,
and our eyes glow
with crystalline beginning.

VOZ DE LA GENTE

I went to river last night,
sat on a sandbar, crosslegged,
played my drum. My third hour,
tum—tum-tum, I noticed four young boys
waist-high in water, quarter mile down river,
staring at me. Tum—tum-tum. . . .
I stared, tum'd louder, stronger,
pads of my hands stung with each slap
on deerskin drum,
sound radiating ancient tribal rap
into night, an ancient heartbeat.
   Where the shore doglegs
   to the middle of the river,
   group of men and women stood.
Their silhouettes
defined in metallic moonlight,
gleaming in brown murky water.
I slapped harder, faster,
wild weed doctor covering night with my cure,
with *matachines* handstep, slow, then fast,
brown notes smoked and misted
close to sleeping children's lips,
curled in their hair, in adobe houses
along La Vega, Vito Romero road, and Atrisco.
   There would be no tomorrow,
   no mountains, no *llano,*
   no me,
and my drum softened its speech to whisper
sleeping to the shores,
singing us all together.
   I heard rattling branches
   crackle
   as thousands of *la gente* pushed through the bosque,
   lining the Río Grande shore.

Standing knee high in water, crowds swooped
out into the shallows,
drawn by the ancient voice of their beginnings.

> Then I awoke.
And now this morning I run five miles
to Bridge street and back,
the dream clings to my ankles like leg-irons
a prisoner drags, and there is a pain
in the pads of my hands
that will not subside,
> > until I play the drum.

BJ

for BJ

Stroke confined
his wife
to the old clapboard house,
he combs her, dresses her, shoulders
her
to the kitchen rocker,
where she sits
next to the fireplace,
smelling favorite soup
waver up
from the blackened pot
on the woodstove top.
After breakfast
BJ goes out to the wet work,
flute of his tractor
grumbling chapters
of cruel weather and hard dirt
lived through,
a burly, black-iron coughing song
of his love for the early morning,
for the earth he worked
seventy-two years.

CUSTOM

for Juan

Juan umphs cinch comfortably taut,
Baby snortles a bit,
Juan swings galvanized gate open,
mounts Baby, fits
straw cowboy hat low over eyes,
clicks tongue, and the small herd of Holsteins
clump lazily out of the back-yard corral
at dawn. It's more than need
or relaxing ride on the *acequia,*
it's an ancient custom ingrained in his blood,
cleaved deep to the oldest center of story-telling days.
His sunburned brown face
is pungent with stillness of custom burned in,
custom left there by grandfather
for the next man in line to take a turn.
Holstein chew ditchbank grass weed,
slog down embankment, hoof-sog muddy
chest brimming current, tongue daub
black snouts, then lope up, bogged, matted wet,
shivering hide-roars of raindrops on air.
They move on same path for years,
with the measure of a man
slowly sipping canteen water as he crosses the desert.
Juan swats straw hat on thigh,
lumpy soft with years of wear and sweat.
Baby's saddle bags packed with jalepeños,
tortillas, bottled water, bulge with nonchalant
rub of leather on leather with each step.
Cattle mosey on, mill groggily under cottonwood shade,
shred bankweed   loll   yank grass   move on
while Juan sits proudly in his saddle
waving at friends passing by,
and smokes a self-rolled cigarette in the shade.

— 87 —

Clicks tongue, Baby's ears perk, cowlick fluff of
rough shaggy cedar-bark, and she gives knee-high
step. The lugubrious scrawl of cattle
plod on, their pace history heavy
creaks earth roots.

Jogging on the ditchbank,
I come up to him—
silver clippings of halter tarnished by years'
hoof dust and Baby's foamy sweat,
stirrups burnished, grooved by boots,
tasseled saddle worn down by his weight,
shell-buttoned cowboy shirt faded,
and I ask him, "Bet if you were on a cliff,
and wanted her to jump, she'd jump."
He pats her neck, "She sure would, my old sweet Baby."

EL SAPO

for Frog King

Around the bend on Black Mesa Loop,
Sapo lived. Dirt driveway
shadowed with arbored trees,
curving to his front door.
Este viejo was *el más firme*
en to'l mundo.
Un gordo, sin miedo. . . .
Every time I went to see him
he was sitting in his massive E-Z-Boy recliner,
his greeting always expectant
for a *movida.*
I always offered an impossible scheme
for getting money.
He didn't care about the money
as much as he did about the lovely energy,
the raw impulse of human nature
to forge out something
through courage and daring
rather than meek security.
He wanted to take chances.
He wanted to gamble.
Once his Great Danes rambled off
and bit some farmer's dogs.
He gave his Danes to the farmer.
He said, "I wanna be buried under a rock
when I die." Then he laughed. He always laughed
with a voice that sounded like a growl,
a rough-edged animal purr
filled with wilderness lust.

He didn't covet life,
he didn't protect his life from wind,
from earth,

from the badness of thieves
or sweetness of saints. If his soul were a thousand trees,
he wrapped it around mountains.

He loved testing man's hope,
man's faith in himself to be courageous.
To him, loyalty was half of life.
The other half was breaking boundaries,
pushing extremes,
chancing the great hovering darkness
of the unknown.

He was robust,
extravagant and extraordinary.
Bred from tractor smoke and rows of tobacco,
his laughter rustled deeply,
corn leaves in windy afternoon,
his exuberance for life
flower-topped alfalfa opening to sun
and harvesting blades. To him, good
with bad. If you couldn't take one,
then don't expect the other.

He drank white liquor,
left in a jar on the porch a year.
Spoke words full of fire, clean white fire from the heart,
made space glow with human radiance.

His character rolled from him
wide-open space and hills.
His face ruddy with cold weather and labor,
emanating a love for dirt roads, one-car bridges
iced over, snowy nights spent stranded in his truck cab
on the side of the road,
wild-hearted women, cigar-smoldering rooms in mountain cabins.
and endless hours of poker.

He loved life, loved people,
consumed them both with unending passion.

I remember he had
a coffin for a livingroom table.
He laughed with a carefree shrug
at death. Veins puffed out
of his great swollen turtle feet,
and he moved with ancient grace
his three hundred pounds
on gnawed heels of old toe-slumped boots.
Chipped and battered, he lived
serenely above tree-choked ponds.
In a blue farmer's feedstore baseball cap,
faded khakis, hay-smelling jacket,
his gray-brown tousled hair,
his skin tough as turtle hide,
his eyes glinting a cunning pleasure
at living.

He loved life!
When he clambered in his blue pickup,
heaving his great body
            in and resting his foot sideways on the gas pedal,
            with a great avalanche of voice,
            filling cab space smelling of hot upholstery,
Frog King would say, his voice
sand's dark moist underbelly,
speckled and gritted with black dirt, Sapo would say,
"Well, come on, goddamn." His growlish laughter
purring in his chest and eyes.
            His big hands rusty-hard with work
            carried the weight
            of old tractor blades
            that had moved and ploughed up tons of dirt
            in their time.

— 91 —

His soul was an iron bell,
clapper struck and worn down and cracked
by friends constantly calling at all hours,
every day, for years.
He was his own church
and the religious teachings he believed in
unfolded in green leaves,
fuzzy mornings of fog-sheeping pastures,
black bulls
muzzling hilltop clover and grass,
big strong dogs,
dusty country roads—
       when the dawn struck Sapo's eye
       these things
       throbbed, clanged and drummed the ground.

And yet some disliked him,
closed their ears to his rough music,
his raw singing of body and heart.
These people wore
white gloves over their hearts,
unsoiled by his dusty laughter.
Their souls cracked in attics,
in picture frames,
in family trunks. These
people afraid of his humanity,
hummed with warm-motor hearts,
blood pulsed colored blinking lights,
whose days were constant tapes and ribbons
of information.
A man like Sapo,
short-circuited their heaven,
his root-charged blood darkened their ivory nails and cracked
       their glass flowers.

They clawed his broad shoulders and tried
to bring him down,

to choke his husky neck
with editorial pens and
silver-needle glares,
with laws and threats,
but as always he treated their illnesses
with no more attention
than the bark of a pine tree
attends to beetles.

He could care less if you were rich or poor
or colored. He laughed at all the stupid prejudices
and presumptions of people.
You were either a man or not.
"Goddamn," he would say, when something surprised him.
"Goddamn, you no good son of a bitch," was his way
of saying he liked you.
He squabbled, arguing for a penny
on a used car.
With an eye on people the way migrating cranes
eye topography and know what they know, he knew life and people.

It's not sad that you died, Sapo.
I regret not having seen you
before you died.

It shook me up
when I heard you died.
I didn't think the gods could take you.
I got the letter.
I said, "How could he die?"
A sledge hammer crushed my skull.
I said, "Shit! How can such a good man die?"
I wasn't ready. I was caught off guard.
Good thing I didn't show for your funeral.
I probably would have jumped
in the grave, opened the coffin,
and shook you awake, both of us wrestle-laughing

with the mourners. We probably
would have drank for days straight
seeing the joke we pulled on everyone,
and settled on an oak stump,
scratching up handfuls of black earth
from time to time, kissing it,
getting dirt grains on our tongues,
feeling the gritty brown taste,
washed it down with bootleg liquor,
and started cursing at gods, yours and mine,
for not letting us argue over one last used car,
over whether ghosts were real or not,
over women.

Your blood is red country-road mud,
your veins paths curving into
brushy thickets of forest darks.

When I was around you
darkness stilled in me,
and I'd get lost in all the freedom.
My words with you had to be honest,
strike sparks off the two pieces of flint
we were. We invented our fire.
'Cause where we went, we couldn't take
anything but our nakedness, our honesty,
our sheer love of being wild and untamed.
Every day was mating season for you.
And how you loved young bucks
swelling their nostrils,
lowering their antlers,
wrangling with you.
It wasn't winning or losing, but the grunting
gut-aching laughter.

A stuffed python curled on your tv,
rifles and guns friends pawned you
in the spare bedroom, white liquor

in the cabinet below the kitchen sink
in gallon milk jugs, an old grandfather clock
you shattered once leaning back on the E-Z-Boy too far,
a writing desk, bullets in ash trays—
your house a great American pawn shop,
thieves, senators and poets,
governors, pimps, and widows came to
to bite a slice of moon,
and sip a glass of sunlight
with you, who never gave a damn for nothing.
You were a sensuous man.
Pleasure was a bullet that took your life.
Your horse-trading gambling talk
convinced a woman to sell her husband,
persuaded another he could run naked
before the police station without being caught,
and another he could swim across the Pacific
in winter. On every one you bet.

You didn't wait for life,
didn't limit it to certain hours.
You tore the rule book up
that depicted a family, a man in a suit,
children playing with blocks,
a back yard, sidewalks, bills, a shiny car.
For you it was coming and going
as you pleased, spending what you pleased,
saying what you felt,
rearing like a wild horse caught in a dead-end canyon.
When you had to act the gentleman,
you trampled the cowboys over,
dragged their loose rope ends behind you,
hell, you were quite a man Sapo,
quite a man.

I see you now—
listening to Gods sitting on tree stumps
telling you stories

you find hard to believe.
You help those old men
and women get up, hold
their arms as they lean on you,
and you help them cross the roads of white stars,
leading them carefully to their homes in black endless space.

You loved poetry, loved poetry.
You genuinely loved poetry.
So this one's for you, Sapo.

NEWS

Just drove back from town,
I walk down the road
to hear the latest news.
On the porch with other men,
Dennis, a migrant with a Texas twang,
tells his version,
"We knew it,
but not this bad, lord no.

Land wrinkled up
squinting at the clouds,
and them fine fat rows
got thin as an old woman."
(He took a drink. Wiped his lips.)

"That heat came on
angry as a wet hen,
and when the heat hit the cold
lord, lord. Some darkening it got,
put that sky damn black.
Started over that way. I seen it come,
hail big as golf balls and small apples.
Looked like someone took an ax
and hacked them chili leaves
right clean. Stalks looked like stakes,
es all like that.

"Doggonit,
leaves stacked feet deep in the road
front of Baca's house. And Chambers
standing there, looking out the window.

"I came out round that pond back there.
No need to go mo, by god,

Padilla's field was plum flat.
It turned, came round them Arabs' store,
stomping corn and rag'n leaves.

"Lots of crying in kitchens,
I tell you, es all they could do.
Took them crops, and not single one
'm boys had insurance.

"I went up by Pete's meadow
one we cleared some years ago.
Back behind them woods. That's right.
Pete was there sitting in his truck,
drinking by himself. Didn't need
to see no mo.

Went on down Chavez store
and filled me a mason jar with whiskey.
Everytime that wind hit, blew chairs
off porch and knocked porchswing
'gainst wall and ceiling, I'd take a drink.
Lord no, didn't need no wind and rain like that."

I walked down the road, no need
to turn on the tv for the evening news.

A FIELD OF CLOVER

for Evelyn

Evelyn dreamed
both of you running
through a field of clover
before you died, Joe.

After you and Evelyn
painted kitchen cabinets and trim-boards
with flowers,
you died.

Evelyn
is a woman in the garden
by herself now. Each gem stone
you worked on the grinder
in your garage
she has carefully set
in the garden
of her heart. She walks
the dazzling cobbled path
each morning.

The world is a broken gate.
She is an old woman
who cannot fix it anymore.
She has a soreness in her bones
she cannot rub away,
a soreness at the far edge
of her heart,
posted
Keep Out.
Days brawl and scuffle
like gulls for scraps of her life.

She scrapes and butts the pier
of each night like a battered boat,
her heart
a lump of gray, sleepy sails.
She would move to Arizona,
but she stays to care for her
mother. On weekends at her mother's house,
a shade-laced clapboard
skirted by oak trees,
she spends her afternoons.

Over the flowers you both painted,
another winter
wilts the tulips, scabs the roses,
where the old woman walks.
On evenings, in her armchair,
poodle in lap, Evelyn's eyes
blur more and more of this life out,
and she remembers the dream—
her eyes become clear
and clearer with the picture
of you both running in a field of clover.

INFLUENCES

I have missed so much of life,
my face like a doormat, has so often seen the undersoles of
travelers' shoes and boots, smelled the greens and dirts in
their cleats, and I have spent a life imagining their travels.

TOWARD THE LIGHT

Few inches beneath
ground surface,
my son heel'd up
a frog.
It died in leap.
Crook't brittle hook-hands,
scoop of dirt beneath
its black flecked belly.
        Nostril slits
        flared
to the faint warmth of spring,
back legs shoved
at dense dirt, pushed, pushed,
up, up, 'til exhausted old
miner let
legs and arms go limp,
small toes
fanned out a last back-dirt scoop,
then it rested its broad gullet
down gravely, severe-mouthed,
and died in a grimaced leap at light
an inch above.
        I pick it up,
            sand grains
tick inside hollow shell,
eyelids dark scars, blunted snub nose.
Olmec King
unearthed by my son's sneaker
I enthrone in my baseball cap,
bring home, set next
to other desk-top jewels—
        Monarch butterfly,
        obsidian stone,
        piñons, pine cones,

pebbles, eagle feather,
withered rose bud,
robin's egg,
tuft of sparrow's nest cotton—
welcome Olmec King
welcome,
to my humble museum,

where each thing conveys
an aspect of my own journey.

TOMÁS LUCERO

I wept when the police escorted you to the train.
For years, when the train darkly whipped across the *llano*
at midnight, shuddering my cot, the trembling ground
was your voice still mourning your brother
killed in your yard by the police.
I wept when your small son was engulfed in a blast of steam,
as the Santa Fe train chugged off he stood there,
choking, breast heaving with tears, a dark small shadow
in ghostly smoke.

You have given me hope, Tomás.
I knew you were not a strong man. When you knelt
clutching your bloody brother in your front yard,
across from my house, I saw
how you wept, begging the blood back, the bullet holes healed,
the terrible nightmare erased. The dark cloudy features
of your face were an omen—
            you looked up at the policeman,
            took your brother's gun and shot him—
because of that one tragic moment
you had to become who you were not.
Sniff air, a hunted coyote,
try to charm the moon—
now hunted, you held alien weight of your brother's gun
in your hands
instead of your son's little body,
now earth became your bed, *arroyos* your paths,
instead of your wife's arms,
now you rest on canyon rockrim that overlooks
Estancia, Tajíque, and Willard.
You must have wept for a return, to just sit on your porch,
watch your children playing in the yard
as you scold your oldest son for trampling chile plants
in the garden.

We sent you food, and every day
I have walked to your house to see how your family is doing.
When the police came to ask of you,
our silence asked them to leave our yard.

When you were finally caught,
I looked into your son's face
watching you embark the train for prison.
I saw the most beautiful, inexpressible love and adoration
burst over and effuse his sorrowful face.
And then months after, a mysterious nobility
filled his eyes, two dark wounds bleeding your image
on everything they looked on—
Never have I seen anything as beautiful, Tomás,
as your son who is becoming a man.

BEDTIME STORY TO THE BOYS

I lie in bed and they run after me,
jump onto the bed, and cry,
"Tell us a story, Papi!"

What we did together
turns into a magical story

"A man builds a patio. Two little boys
dig next to Papi. They find
a worm, which decided to turn
into a butterfly, big as their hands.
'How are you, little boys?'
Butterfly asks. Little boys close
their eyes and butterfly
takes them down into earth,
to its home. Things shine.
'Those are baby suns,' Butterfly says,
'when they are ready they will walk the long
journey cross the earth. Work to shine. . . .' "

My sons' eyes heavy-lidded
from the glow, slowly close.
They dream they are throwing baby suns
in the air, skipping after them,
as they roll across the street,
then sail upward, floating past
tenement windows of wakeful parents,
watching David Letterman show,
the bubble machine. . . .

ON BLOOD AND BONE

Antonio awakens, waddles
from bed to livingroom,
cuddles in massive Apache quilt
on couch
to watch morning cartoons.

With levis on, two socks, sneakers,
pullover, long-sleeved red cotton shirt,
light frayed autumn jacket,
awake since six a.m.,
I come out of my office.
"I need a kiss," and he kisses my cheek.

I sit watching Goofy.
This morning the poem in me
is stuck, an old wagon stuck in *caliche*
up to the axles. I wanted to
ride the wagon to a pueblo
far from here, where dreams could greet me
like plump doormen in the cartoon.

"Need another kiss,
to make the machine work right."
As if my body had fallen
into rusty immobility, I crane down
stiffly to kiss his smiling lips,
after which he says,
"Silly Papi, not motors,
we walk on blood and bone."
          The phrase
unearths a great bell
and rings in the ruins
of my rationality.

WIND

Morning darkened by a light night rain.
The earth is an old tattered attic trunk,
which the wind, the furiously howling, slapping wind, last night,
returned to claim—a penitent criminal son
who found he had interited the curse of damnation.
That was the wind last night.
This morning, landscape
is in a heaved disorder. Behind tool shed
a blue quietness in the field,
an unshaven drunkard's face, heavy with sunlit silence,
having loved so thoroughly the night before,
whose hands, broke, shoved, grappled and pushed
with exhausting lust,
with wind.

SEPTEMBER

for Andrew

I browse the chill fields and notice again
how September has its own features.
Roadside weeds vanish
and what's left, stubbling gulches and mounds,
purples and goldens.
Briars are beggars dragged by winds.
Smooth sweeps of small hills like brown bears
settle deep in themselves.

Neon lights down Central
glare garishly black/green/yellow/red.
It's the first week in September
when people's cars idle to warm up,
and closets are opened for trusty coats.
Fast food stand windows
glisten and blink traffic outside.
I look at the reflection of my face,
in the colorful lights and remember

my out-law rapping
night-hustling years, my life
a steaming hot geyser
of formless chaos, fizzling down streets
like hydrochloric acid eats
at sandstone.

I was trying to find myself
in these fluorescent lights.
Binges I threw trying to ease
the madness in me, the confusion
of where I was going to go in this life,
in the immense push-n-shove
of unemployed dream-seekers, black flecks

of burnt dreams constricting my throat
with panic of unknown future, my life reduced
to ultimate nightly risk—
                     "Sir, your order is ready."

I drive home, two boxes
of tamales and burritos on the seat.
I think of Lalo, still playing the deadly game
of copping heroin, Manuel
drinking at bars, gun in waist under his shirt.
Strange fires burn in their eyes.

                     Part of me died
with them. I am a cottonwood
lightning struck and scorched,
a black heart in the trunk. But part of me
still blossoms.
Between cottonwood branches
in my back yard, the moon hangs,
full of bullet holes we shot in it,
looking for our dream.

FALL

Somber hue diffused on everything.
　　　　Each creature, each emptied corn stalk,
　　　　　is richly bundled in mellow light.
In that open unharvested field of my own life,
I have fathered small joys and memories.
My heart was once a lover's swing that creaked in wind
of these calm fall days.
Autumn chants my visions to sleep,
and travels me back into a night
when I could touch stars and believed in myself. . . .

Along the way, grief broke me,
　　　　my faith became hardened dirt
　　　　walked over by too many people.
My heart now, as I walk down this dirt road,
on this calm fall day,
　　　　is a dented
　　　　tin bucket
　　　　filled with fruits
　　　　picked long ago.
　　　　It's getting harder
　　　　to lug the heavy bucket.
　　　　I spill a memory on the ground,
　　　　it gleams,
　　　　rain on hot embers
　　　　of yellow grass.

I AM HERE

for Jaime

I stopped my car on Gibson avenue,
alongside the T-Bird Lounge, and asked
two policemen clubbing a drunk to stop.
>   I was booked
>   for obstruction of justice.
In the back seat with the drunk,
his grimy polyester coat
padded with wads of want-ads,
smelling of dog spittle and trashbins,
his eyelids cracked open
from their concrete numbness,
and his trembling hand reached
for an invisible styrofoam cup
of black coffee on the floor mat.
He gummed thirsty lips
for a small postponement, just a sip,
he dreamed, as we passed liquor stores.

Behind bars, I stand
peering down into tiers.
Porters mill
leaning on mops and brooms.
Chicano in another cell
wears sunglasses
like ancestors wore their war paint.
Christ crucified across chest,
dragon on left arm
twirls through a trellis haze
of vines and roses.
Believer of blood duels,
faith that earth will crack someday
and Aztec warriors rise
to judge the heartless.
He whistles through branches of bars,

hand signing a friend
for brown powder to fertilize
vines of his veins
and make the rose bloom.

Tier guard
stands in front of my cell,
American flag
patched to shoulder above v-rank,
walkie-talkie dangling
from wide black leather belt,
brass buttons and silver badge
painstakingly
polished to impress authority.
"Charges been dropped! You're out! Come on!"
I follow the guard
to the end of the tier,
to a button-paneled cage
where a guard sprawls
like a fat wolf
reading a comic.

From a dark cell
as if from the hull of a slave ship,
I emerge into blinding noon deck-streets,
where sun hacksaws tin sheets of glistening air.

An unblinking anger
fills me. I stare
at strange pedestrians
returning from lunch to the office,
and a cut-checked anger burns my face,
anger that mumbles the world's end
                              over my bones.

I spent the rest of the afternoon
walking familiar streets.
            I withdraw and walk in a place

inside myself, trudging across fierce red sands
of my heart,
                    and through the *arroyos,* sliding down,
turning over small rocks, patiently, searching
for something to describe me. . . .
                              I am here—
                    brown body, blood, bones,
living at Black Mesa outside of Burque.

                                        To Them, I am found,
tagged with a number,
photographed cataloged
". . . fearless . . . violent prone. . . ."
"Mau-Mau warrior," one snickered
an aside.
Outlawed   in Their eyes,
to swing   Their picks,
to be jailed   in Their jails.

I am here, scared, loving, helpful, brave,
graying hair, meditative brown eyes, kind
smile, angry eyes burning for equality.

        I am here.

A BETTER LIFE

My life is a lover's breathing
on embers of dreams
for a better life.
In Juarez when La Migra detained me
in jail for months,
when American jails armored my flesh
with steel skin,
I rejected their iron/concrete skins
for my own
embers of a dream
for a better life.

Dreams do not corrode or rust
like the gun in an officer's hand
or the knife of a violent man,
nor extinguish their pleasure
like tourists
who buy and sell children for sexual play.

Instead,
where there is nothing to believe in,
when I am desperate
and see no future for me,
then my life
is a lover's breathing
on embers of a dream
for a better life.

A DAILY JOY TO BE ALIVE

No matter how serene things
may be in my life,
how well things are going,
my body and soul
are two cliff peaks
from which a dream of who I can be
falls, and I must learn
to fly again each day,
or die.

Death draws respect
and fear from the living.
Death offers
no false starts. It is not
a referee with a pop-gun
at the starting line
of a hundred yard dash.

I do not live to retrieve
or multiply what my father lost
or gained.

I continually find myself in the ruins
of new beginnings,
uncoiling the rope of my life
to descend ever deeper into unknown abysses,
tying my heart into a knot
round a tree or boulder,
to insure I have something that will hold me,
that will not let me fall.

My heart has many thorn-studded slits of flame
springing from the red candle jars.
My dreams flicker and twist

on the altar of this earth,
light wrestling with darkness,
light radiating into darkness,
to widen my day blue,
and all that is wax melts
in the flame—

I can see treetops!

BLACK MESA

for Rito

The northern most U-tip
of Chihuahua desert
infuses
my house
with its dark shadow,
and leans my thoughts
in its direction
as wind bends a row of trees
toward it.

I want to visit
it
before winter comes,
and balance myself
across culvert that connects
my field
to Isleta Pueblo.
Strings of water trellis
from rusty holes
and bubble scum and black moss weed
below.
Branches barrage the passage,
and draw blood at my shoulder
as I crouch past,
then climb No Trespassing fence.

I don't know what this year has meant to me,
but I've come here to find a clue.
Up Black Mesa's east side,
'dozed in '68
to run I-25 south.
Sky showered stones
at children playing

on ditchbanks,
dynamite blasts cracked porches,
foundations, and walls
with shuddering volts.

Rito was murdered here
by sheriffs,
brown beret Chicano activist
who taught children in the barrio
our own history,
tried to stop
them blasting Black Mesa.
And now, under my hiking boots his blood
crossbeds minerals
and forms into red crystals,
ceremonial Chac-Mool plate
on which Aztec warrior Rito
sacrificed his heart to the Sun.

Rito believed in a justice
whose history
is without margins.

To my right, a steep downdrift
gush of cutting boulders,
the jagged edges of a key
that opens my dark life
and gives it a certain meaning
of honor and truth.

I re-imagine myself here,
and pant the same breath
squeezed from these rocks 1000 years ago.

Etched on slabs,
wolf and coyote wear
skins of stone,

watch me pass, silent
at the shortness of my life, at my
brief visit here on earth.
I finger the rough braille
of each drawing
in the cool crevice slab,
and discover in this seeming destruction
a narrative of love
for animals and earth.
I go on,
climb boulders drained
down a rip gorge,
and stand on the flat cap rim
of Black Mesa, fuzzed
with chaparral, cacti and weeds.

In lava cracks,
I learn to read, smell and hear
the darkness again 'til black depths
lighten slowly to twilight
and the old man who lives
in stone
offers me a different view
of life and death.

I believe that whatever tragedy
happens in my life, I can stand on my feet
again and go on.

I lay on a slab stone
and nap in sunlight
unafraid of snakes that plume stones
around me.

In sluggish revery
I am in a small café
in Española.

Seat myself at a round wooden table.
A man approaches me,
sits across from me, and states,
            "Thank you for the stone in my mind.
            It sings to me and I still listen to it."

I rub sun glare from my eyes and look around,
as if he sat next to me,
then walk over to the black-lipped rim rock.
Languid white washed adobe houses below are
obscured by lush branches.
I bend
and pocket a lava chip as token
of my ascent from stone,
                        and go.

I have a vision of mountain range
proportions,
to speak the heart's language.
To write the story of my soul
I trace in the silence and stone
of Black Mesa.

My hope breaks this hour's crust
and ferments
into tomorrow's darkness, into
another year of living,
to evolve with the universe,
side by side with its creative catastrophe.

SANCTUARY

for Tony

I could not dissengage my world
from the rest of humanity.
Wind chill factor 11° below. All night
wind thrashes barechested trees
like a West Texas tent evangelist
            hissing them on their knees,
            lisping
                        sinnn . . . sinn . . . sinn. . . .
                All night wind preaches.
Old tool shed
behind my house
fist-cuffs itself to nail-loose tin,
horse pasture gates
clank their crimes,
while neighing black stallions of rain
stampede on the patio
fleeing gunshots of thunder. . . .

Miles south of here,
nightscopes pick up human heat
that green fuzz helicopter
dash panels.
            A mother whispers,
    "Sssshhhh mejito, nomás poco más allá.
                        Nomás poco más allá."
Dunes of playing-dead people
jack rabbit under strobe lights
and cutting whack/blades,
            "Ssshhh mejito.
            Sssshhhh." Child whimpers
            and staggers in blinding dust
            and gnashing wind.

Those not caught, scratch sand up
to sleep against underbellies
of roots and stones.

Eventually Juanito comes to my door,
sick from eating stucco chips—
his meals scratched off
walls of temporary shelters,
and Enrique, who guzzled water
at industrial pipes
pouring green foam out
at the El Paso/Juarez border,
and Maria steaming with fever,
face dark meteorite, whispers,
> "Where I come from, Señor Baca,
> a woman's womb is a rock,
> and children born from me,
> drop like stones, to become dust
> under death squad's boots."

And Juanito,
> "They came at midnight
> and took my brothers. I have
> never seen them since. Each judge's tongue
> is a bleeding stub of death, and each lawyer's
> finger a soft coffin nail."

And Enrique,
> "You can trust no one.
> Each crying person's eye is a damp cellar
> where thieves and murderers sleep."

They have found refuge here
at Black Mesa.

The sun passes between our lives,
as between two trees,
one gray, one green,
but side by side.

Glossary

Acequía: irrigation ditch
Arroyo: a dry wash usually created by flash floods
¡Aquí vienen!: here they come

Cabron: bastard
Caliche: clay
¡Canta, mujer!: sing, woman!
Con duende: with spirit. *Duende* is an obscure spirit that overtakes the
    individual, who is subsequently plunged into the immediacy of the
    moment. Creator of its own dictates, *duende* constitutes a compelling
    world of its own; it is an existential eternity that infuses a person
    with the joyful sense of living for that one present moment. *Duende*
    has the capacity of spontaneously calling forth and moving the indi-
    vidual to total expression and of manifesting itself with unconscious
    energy in the form of a dance, song, demeanor or attitude.
Curandero: folk healer

El más firme: he with the most compassion and courage, a trustwor-
    thy friend or spiritual brother who won't vacillate in a crisis
Este viejo: this old man
En to'l mundo: contraction of *en todo el mundo*, i.e., in all the world

Hijo de su pinche madre: bastard without mother or father
Horno: a round earthen oven or fireplace

La gente: the people

Llano: the plains
Llano vaqueros: cowboys of the plains

¡Mátalo! ¡Mátalo!: Kill him! Kill him!
Matachines: folk dancers who bless the waters and the earth. At seasonal rituals they celebrate religious and folk customs by dancing and singing. They dress in masks and colorful costumes.
Matanza: a barrio social event where people gather to talk and eat, involving butchering and dressing an animal and, usually, but not always, focusing on an event—Cinco de Mayo, a baptism, etc.
Mejito: contraction of *mi hijito,* a term of endearment for a male child
Mi Tío Baca el Poeta de Socorro: My Uncle Baca the Poet from Socorro
Movida: a hustle

Nichos: a niche in the wall, usually for a small religious or folk statue
Nomás poco más allá: just a little bit further

Ristra: a braided string of *chiles* (peppers)

Santos: folk statues

Terrón: mud bricks cut from the riverbed

Un gordo, sin miedo: a fat guy, with no fear

Vigas: rough wooden ceiling beams, usually of pine
Voz de la gente: voice of the people

New Directions Paperbooks—A Partial Listing

For complete listing request free catalog from
New Directions, 80 Eighth Avenue, New York 10011   †Bilingual